すべて世のため、後のために
塙保己一とヘレン・ケラー

堺正一／文　吉澤みか／絵

はじめに（ヘレン・ケラーが心の支えとした日本人）

　多くの偉人伝が出版されていますが、目も、耳も、ことばも不自由だったアメリカの女性ヘレン・ケラーは、その代表的な人物の一人です。

　重度の障害者であるヘレンが3度も日本を訪れています。昭和12（1937）年の最初の訪問は、すでに57歳のときでした。「人生わずか50年」といわれた時代です。サンフランシスコから、日本の〝浅間丸〟に乗り、15日間の船旅の疲れをいやす間もなく、東京・渋谷の温故学会（塙保己一史料館）を訪問しました。

　つづいて、その感動を胸に浦和の埼玉会館で講演をし、満員の聴衆に向かって、こう話しだしました。

　「わたしは挫折しそうになるたびに、塙保己一先生のことを思いだして、立ち直ることができました。そして、現在のわたしがあるのです。いつか日本に行き、わたしの人生の目標である塙先生の故郷の埼玉を訪問したいと思っていましたが、今日その願いがかないました」

　実は、ヘレンは子どものころから、母親にこの日本の盲目の学者のことを聞かされて大きくなったのです。母親は、いつも、こう話してくれました。

　「日本には、幼いときに失明したのに、努力してりっぱな学者になった〝塙保己一〟という先生がいます。点字も盲学校もない時代、本を読んでもらって、暗記するほかはありませんでした。でも、あなたはちがいます。自分で読み書きできる点字もあるし、盲学校や聾学校もあります。それに、いつもそばにいて、助言してくれる家庭教師のサリバン先生がいるではありませんか。つらいことがあっても、塙先生のことを思いだしてがんばりましょうね」

＊

明治時代には、この少女のことは日本の教育界にも伝えられ、「どんなに重い障害があっても、教育の機会が保障されさえすれば、ひとりの人間としてりっぱに成長できる」ことが証明され、大きな話題になりました。

それでは、ヘレン・ケラーが人生の目標とし、こころの支えとした日本人とは、どんな人物だったのでしょうか？

※塙保己一の名は、一生の間に何度も変わっている。混乱をさけるために、この本では、子ども時代は「辰之助」、江戸に出て学問を始めるまでを「千弥」、学問の道に進んでからは「塙保己一」と表記した。

講演で塙保己一への思いを話すヘレン・ケラー。

目のお医者さま

　武蔵国（現在の埼玉県、東京都、神奈川県の一部）の北のはて、現在の埼玉県本庄市児玉町の農家の長男に生まれた辰之助（のちの塙保己一）が目を病みながらも、まだ見えていたころのことです。

　家から2里（約8km）も離れた上野国の藤岡村（現在の群馬県藤岡市）まで、母親に手を引かれて、治療に通っていました。目の治療で評判の医者の名は桐渕幸助といい、俳諧（現代の俳句）を好み、学問を愛する人でもありました。

　正月も過ぎ、雪をかぶった浅間山を遠くに見ながら、母親に手を引かれてやって来た幼い辰之助に、桐渕先生は優しく声をかけてくれるのでした。

　「辰之助はえらい、えらい！　北風に負けずによく来たね」

　お医者さまは、母親に手を引かれ、冷たい空っ風のなかを、顔を真っ赤にしてやって来た辰之助の手を、あたたかい手でつつんであげるのでした。そして、

　「辰之助の好きな食べ物はなにかな？」

　「つみっこ！　あったかくって、おいしいんだ」

　「ちょうどよかった。わしらも、いま食べたところだが、よかったら、お母さんといっしょに少し食べないか？　体があったまるぞ」

　〝つみっこ〟は、地元で採れた小麦と野菜をたっぷり使った郷土料理の〝すいとん〟のことです。昔から小麦の栽培と養蚕が盛んなこの地方では、仕事の合間や寒い季節によく食べられていました。

　「先生、ごちそうさま！　おいしかったね、お母ちゃん」

　「よかったね、辰之助。寒いときには何よりのごちそうで……、この子もひたいに汗をかいていますよ」

おいしそうに〝つみっこ〟をほおばる辰之助。

「辰之助、ここに来る途中、お百姓さんは畑で何をしていたかな？」

「みんな〝麦踏み〟をしていたよ。おいらもお母ちゃんの麦踏みの手伝いをしているんだ。踏んであげないと〝つみっこ〟にするいい麦はできないんだよね。ねっ、お母ちゃん」

「辰之助、なぜ麦踏みをするのか、知っているかい？」

「麦踏みしてあげないと、寒さに負けない強い麦になれないんだ。踏んであげると霜や北風にも負けなくなるんだ」

「よくわかっているね。小さな麦を踏むのはかわいそうな気がするけど、そうしないと良い粒が実らない。だから、小さいうちに三度も四度も踏んであげるんだ。人間だって同じこと……なんども踏みつけられて、苦しいことがあるかもしれないけど、そのたびに、たくましくなるということを忘れ

てはいけないよ。寒いからといって、囲炉裏のまわりにばかりいては強い子になれんぞ」

「先生、おいら、だいじょうぶだよ。〝子どもは風の子〟だもん！」

「……お母さん、辰之助は賢い子だ。〝心の目〟とでもいうのか……、〝見えないからこそ気づく大切なもの〟があるのだろう」

それからというもの、辰之助は「苦しい思いをするたびに、それだけたくましくなれる」というお医者さまのことばを忘れずに、冷たい空っ風のなかを、麦踏みを手伝うのでした。

しかし、5歳になるころには医者通いのかいもなく、辰之助の目は、ほとんど見えなくなっていたのです。

医者から「再び見えるようにはならないだろう」と聞かされ、両親は辰之助の将来を心配し、途方にくれるのでした。

おかあさんの横で、楽しそうに麦踏みをする辰之助。

手習い師匠は和尚さま

　この日も、辰之助の家の裏手に
ある龍清寺の寺子屋から子どもた
ちの元気な声が聞こえてきます。
　縁側でぼんやりと日向ぼっこを
している息子を見ていた母親は
　「辰之助も手習い＊がしたいで
しょうに……。かわいそうで、涙
が出ますよ。この子のことを、和
尚さまにお願いできないでしょう
かねぇ、お父さん」
　「母さんの気持ちはわかるが、
目が見えないのだから和尚さまを
困らせるだけだろう……。辰之助
にはかわいそうだがな」
　　　　　　＊
　ある日、杖をたよりに龍清寺の
カヤの木陰にやってきた辰之助
が、そっと寺子屋の様子をうか
がっています。その姿に気づいた
和尚さまは声をかけました。
　「辰之助や、こっちへ来て、
いっしょに手習いをしないか？」

＊江戸時代の寺子屋で行われていた教育で、文字の読み書きや習字を習うこと。

カヤの木陰から寺子屋の様子をうかがう辰之助に、そっと声をかける和尚さま。

「……和尚さま、辰っちゃんは目が見えねぇんだから、手習いは無理じゃあねぇか？」

「そんなことを言うものじゃないぞ。さあ、辰之助、こっちへ来てあがりなさい」

とまどいながら、杖をたよりに探りよってきた辰之助。うつむきながら、

「でも……、おいら、目が見えないから……」

「気にしなくてもいい。はやくこっちへおいで。……これからは、ここが辰之助の席だ。いいかい、みんな、明日からはここに辰之助を案内してあげるんだぞ」

家でぼんやりとひとりで過ごすよりも、仲間といっしょに話を聞くだけでもよいのでは……と、和尚さまは考えたのです。

和尚さまに案内されて、寺子屋の席につく辰之助。顔には満面の笑みがあふれている。

　こうして、本堂のかたすみに席をもうけてもらった辰之助は、手習いの様子にじっと耳をかたむけるのでした。

　和尚さまは仲間といっしょに　やっていけるか心配したのですが、辰之助は毎日顔を輝かせてやってくるのです。元気をとりもどした辰之助を見て、両親は和尚さまに手をあわせるのでした。

辰之助の笑顔を見てよろこぶ、父親と母親。二人の心のなかは、和尚さまへの感謝の気持ちでいっぱいだ。

ある日、和尚さまは子どもたちに琵琶法師の話をしてくれました。琵琶法師とは、琵琶という弦楽器にあわせて『平家物語』*1を語る、お坊さまの姿をした盲目の芸人のことです。その琵琶法師さながら、声をはりあげて熱演する和尚さまに、子どもたちは大喜びです。

　　祇園精舎の鐘の声、
　　諸行無常の響きあり。
　　沙羅双樹の花の色、
　　盛者必衰の理をあらわす。
　　・・・・・・・・・・・・・・・・・

　辰之助は「おごる平家は久しからず」というこの話にすっかり心を奪われてしまいました。興味ぶかそうに聞き入っている辰之助に気づいた和尚さまは、時間を見つけては、いま江戸で人気の『太平記』*2を少しずつ読み聞かせてくれたのです。

　漢文まじりの難しい話に聞きいっている辰之助は、驚いたことに、そっくりおぼえてしまうのです。そして、家に帰ると両親や近所の年寄りたちを前に、和尚さまの

盲目の琵琶法師の図。弦楽器の琵琶の伴奏で、主に『平家物語』などの軍記物を語る盲目の芸人。

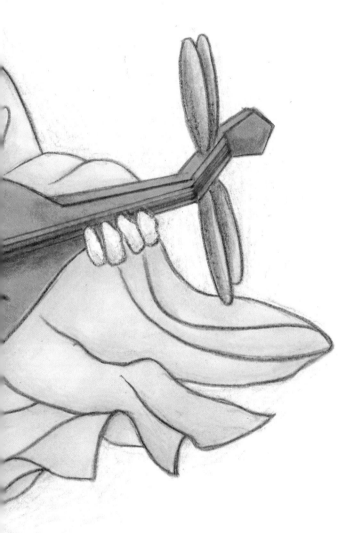

口調までまねて語るのです。村人たちの間でも評判になりました。

　しかし、辰之助は子どもたちの仲間に入れてもらえないこともありました。目が見えないのに、だれよりも学問ができることが、かえって意地悪をされる原因になったのでしょう。そのためか、辰之助の関心は、いっそう学問に向いていったのです。

　「歴史ってなんておもしろいのだろう。和尚さまが読んでくれる『太平記』は40巻もあるそうだけど、いつかはみんなおぼえてしまいたい。盲目の琵琶法師が『平家物語』をおぼえたのなら、自分にもできないはずはない！」

　こうして、和尚さまの手によって、少年の心にまかれた小さな学問の種は芽をふき、風雨にさらされながらも、畑の麦のようにたくましく成長していきました。

＊1　鎌倉時代に盲目の琵琶法師が語るために書かれた物語で、平家の繁栄と没落が描かれている。

＊2　鎌倉時代末期から南北朝時代までの50年余りの合戦の様子が描かれ、江戸時代には、琵琶法師の『平家物語』に代わって、太平記読みという芸人によって大流行した。

江戸へのあこがれと挫折

　辰之助が11歳の夏、母親がかぜをこじらせ、家族の必死のかいほうもむなしく亡くなりました。あっという間のことで、自分が苦労をかけたために、無理がたたったのではないかと辰之助は自分を責めるのでした。

　愛情を注いでくれた母親を亡くし、生きる希望を失いかけていたときのことです。毎年、蚕の繭の買いつけに来る出入りの絹商人が、こんな話をしてくれました。

　「昔から盲人といえば平家琵琶だが、今では江戸では琵琶法師の姿は見かけることも少なくなった。代わって『太平記』を客の前で読み聞かせる"太平記読み"がたいそうな人気で、講釈場（寄席）もあちこちにできて、どこも客でいっぱいだ。辰之助さんが『太平記』を語るのを聞かせてもらったが、見事なものだ。平家琵琶とちがい、盲目の太平記読みの

ことはあまり聞かないが、辰之助さんなら修業しだいで、りっぱにやっていけるだろう」

　これを聞いた辰之助は心をおどらせました。もういても立ってもいられません。

　「和尚さまに読んでもらった『太平記』、……ぜんぶ暗記したいと思っていたやさき……、これほど自分にむいた仕事は、ほかにはないのでは……」

　江戸で『太平記』を語っている自分の姿を想像するのでした。

＊

　知り合いもいない江戸に出たいという盲目の息子を心配して反対していた父親も、辰之助の熱心さに根負けし、「息子の将来に新しい道が開けるなら……」と、江戸に出ることを許したのです。

　こうして、14歳の夏、あの絹商人に手引してもらい、辰之助は江戸に旅立ちました。

着替えなどを入れた木箱（後に"お宝箱"と名づけられた）を風呂敷に包んで背負い、江戸に旅立つ辰之助の後ろ姿。

江戸に出て身を寄せたのは、はり治療で評判の雨富須賀一検校の盲人一座＊でした。入門すると一座の慣例にしたがって髪をそり、名前も〝千弥〟とかえ、新しい生活が始まりました。しかし、江戸での生活は考えていたほど甘くはありませんでした。

　幕府は盲人保護のために、三味線・琴などの芸能、あんま・はりの治療に加えて、座頭金と呼ばれる金貸しに特別な権利を認めていました。

　しかし、千弥はほかの弟子たちとちがい、「〝太平記読み〟になりたい……、ひょっとしたら学問の道にすすめるかもしれない」という淡い望みをいだいて江戸に出てきたのですから興味のないあんまや三味線の修業には身が入りません。

　やる気がおこらなければ上達するはずはないのです。ほかの弟子からは〝怠け者〟とののしられ、とうとう〝むだ飯食い〟とかげ口をきかれるようになってしまいました。千弥は「一座には、もう自分の居場所はない」と思いました。

＊当時の盲人たちは、幕府公認の「当道座」という自治組織をつくり、あんま・はり、琴・三味線・琵琶などの職業訓練をし、経済的にも自立していた。同時にたがいが助け合い生活していく互助組織でもあった。

千弥と名前をかえ、あんまや三味線の修業をするが、まったく身が入らない自分を情けなく感じているようす。

盲人と金貸し（座頭金）

　そんな千弥はある日、兄弟子から貸金の取り立てを言いつけられました。

　「神田三河町の長屋に弥平という大工がいるのだが、一両二分の金を貸してある。今日は利子をそろえて返してもらう日だから、取り立てに行ってこい」

　「……はっ、はい」とは返事をしたものの、気が優しい千弥には貸金の取り立てなど、とても無理なのです。

　千弥はしぶしぶ出かけていったものの、不安はあたりました。食べるのにも困って借金はしたが、今は返す金がないと、妻は平謝りです。

　「申し訳ありません。夫はかぜをこじらせて、仕事に出られず、おまけにこの子まで熱を出し、お医者さまに薬代を払ってしまいました。来月まで待っていただきたいのですが……」

貸金の取り立てに行ったが、返してもらえず、兄弟子から責められて絶望する千弥。

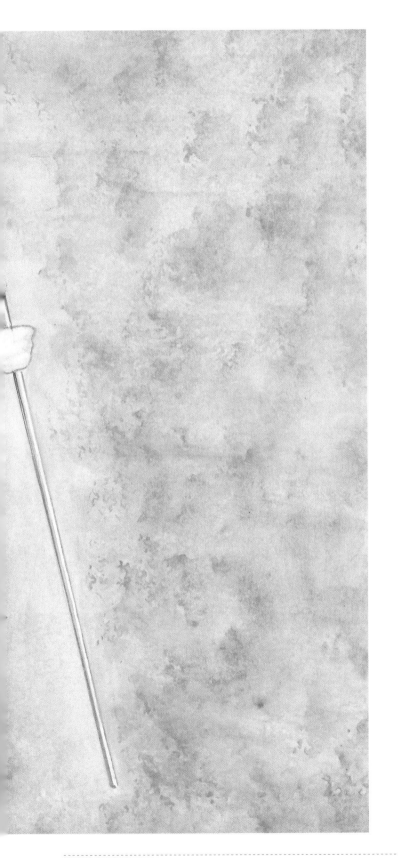

この日は、とうとう貸金は返してもらえず、兄弟子から「役立たず！」と責めたてられました。道具がなければ、職人は働きに出ることも、家族を養うこともできないことを承知のうえで、「道具箱を借金が払えるまで預かっておく」と脅してでも貸した金を返してもらえというのです。高い利息に加えて、情け容赦もない取り立ては世間から恐れられていました。＊

千弥はこんなやり方にはどうしてもついていけないのです。

「このままでは、いつになっても学問などの修業はできないだろう。だからといって、今さら田舎に逃げ帰っては、送り出してくれた村の人たちにあわせる顔がない。いっそのこと、亡くなった母のあとを追って……」

＊盲人一座（当道座）には細かい階級があり、もとは人物、技能によって昇進したのだが、保己一の時代になると、その地位はすべて金で買うようになった。わずかなあんまなどの収入では出世がむずかしく、そこで幕府は盲人保護のために、その金を特別に高利で貸し付けることを認めたのが座頭金。その結果、伝統的な職業を捨てて、金儲けに走る盲人が多く、社会問題になっていた。

愛の巾着袋と一座のお師匠さま

　ある日の昼下がり、千弥は、ほかの弟子たちが出はらうのを見とどけると、そっと屋敷から抜けだしました。行く当てもなく杖をたよりにさまよっていましたが、江戸城のお堀のひとつ、牛ヶ淵まで来ると、ふらふらっと……足をすべらせ、堀に落ちました。もがいていたその手に触れたのは、肌身離さず身に着けていた母の形見の

巾着袋を手に、お堀の水面でもがく千弥の心には、母親の姿が浮かんだ。

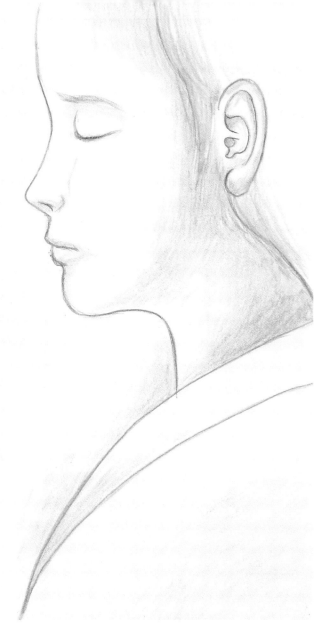

巾着袋でした。そのとき、母の声が耳元でハッキリと聞こえたのです。

「こんなことで、死んではダメ！　お母さんは、そんな弱虫に育てたおぼえはありませんよ。どんなにつらくても、生きるのです！　〝一寸先は光〟＊と教えたでしょ。生きるのですよ！」

気がつくと、どこからか自分の名を呼ぶ声がしました。

「千弥さん！　この帯につかまって、……しっかりつかんでいてくださいよ！」

＊「一寸先は闇」は「少し先のことは何が起こるかわからない」という意味のことわざ。「一寸先は光」ということわざはない。母は少しでも盲目の息子の不安をぬぐおうと、あえて「闇」を「希望の〝光〟」といいかえて話したのだろう。

自分の帯をといて千弥の胸元へ投げてくれたのは、雨富検校の屋敷で下働きをしている和助という初老の男でした。

　和助は千弥を屋敷に連れもどすと、玄関にはいるなり、

「検校さまっ、検校さまっ！」

「……どうしたのだ、和助。落ちつきなさい……」

「落ちついてなんかいられませんや。千弥さんが……。あっしが通りかかったからいいようなものの、とんだことになるところでした。牛ヶ淵に……」

「なっ、なんと……、千弥が身投げを！」

＊

　しばらくして、着替えをすませた千弥がうなだれて、和助と並んで雨富検校の前に座っています。

「和助、話してみなさい」

「……実は、ご用の帰りに、あっしが牛ヶ淵にさしかかると、人の気配がする……。虫が知らせたとでもいうのか、いつもだった

らそのまま通り過ぎるんですが、みょうに気になって、戻ってみたんです。驚いたじゃありませんか。お堀でもがいている男がいる。なんと千弥さんじゃありませんか！　夢中で帯をといて投げてやったというわけなんで……」

「千弥、今も最近のお前のことをどうしたものかと心配していたところだ」

「………………」

「どうして、死のうなどと……。なんでも話してみなさい」

「一年前、反対する父親を説きふせてこの江戸に出て、お師匠さまの弟子にしていただきました。江戸に出れば、盲人でも努力しだいで一人前に生きていける、そう聞いておりましたから……。でも……わたしは何をやってもダメなのです。あんまも三味線も、どうしても興味がわかないのです。だからといって、今さら田舎に帰るわけにもいかず、いっそのこと死んだおっかさんのところに行け

ば、どんなに楽か……気がついたらお堀端に来ていました。あとは、もう……」

「なんということだ！　お前とはいつかゆっくり話さなければ……と思っていたのだが……。今、『死んでしまいたい』と言ったが、それで亡くなったおっかさんが喜ぶとでも思うのかい？　お

やじさんだって同じこと……」

「お師匠さま、………」

「それはそうと、千弥は一体なにをやりたいのだ？　琴や三味線、あんまやはりが、われら盲人に与えられた天職、……だれもが自分に向いたものを見つけて生活をしている。なのに、お前は……」

「みんなわたしが………」

和助に助けられて屋敷にもどった千弥から話を聞く雨富検校。

「だがな、お前はダメな人間ではないぞ。はじめて会ったときから、やる気さえあれば、人並み以上のことができる、……わしは今でも、そう信じている。だが、お前にはやる気が見られないのだ。何をしたいのか言ってみなさい」

「……太平記読みか、……できれば学問が……」

「なっ、なんと言った？　はっきり言いなさい！」

「……あんまの修業をしていても、学問のことが頭から離れないのです。……田舎では、近くの寺の和尚さまから『平家物語』や『太平記』などを読んでいただきました。わたしには、これほどおもしろいものはないのです」

「だがな、自分で読み書きのできない盲人が、いくら好きだからといって、学問では飯を食ってはいけまい」

「むずかしいことはわかっています。でも、学問のためなら、どんな苦労にも耐えられます」

「これまでの千弥には、なに一つ〝これは……〟というものがない。だが、以前、わしが杉山検校さまの医学書を講じたときのことだが、お前の理解力・記憶力、それに集中力には感心した。………困難を覚悟で、学問がしたいというのなら、やりたいことを思いきりやってみるがいい。わしが生活費のめんどうはみよう。……だがな、3年たっても見るべきものがなければ、そのときは児玉の実家に帰すが、それでよいな」

「……あっ、ありがとうございます。破門されてもしかたがないわたしに、好きなことをやってもよいとのお言葉。これからは、……あんまの修業にもはげみます」

「よい、よい。泣くやつがあるか。せいぜいがんばりなさい。もう二度とおかしな考えを起こすのではないぞ。……亡くなったおっかさんや、田舎のおやじさんを悲しませるようなことだけはしないでくれ」

学問を極めたいと考えている千弥に関係する2つのイメージ。ひとつは、学問書。もうひとつは、母親手づくりの形見である木綿の巾着袋。古い木綿の帯を再利用してお守りがわりにつくってくれたもので、保己一は一生涯肌身離さず持ち歩いていたという。

朗読ボランティアに支えられて

　さっそく保己一（千弥から改名）の学問の修業が始まり、こんな評判が広がりました。

　「雨富検校のところの若い弟子が、どこに行くにも、本を持ち歩き、あんまが終わると、わずかな時間をさいてもらって本を読んでもらっているそうだ」

　お金のない保己一には読んでもらったお礼は、あんまでお返しをするほかはありません。ですから、いっしょうけんめい修業に励みました。すると、「あんまの保己一さん」と評判になるほど上達し、ひいきにしてくれる人たちもふえていったのです。

　そのころ、あんまの値段は、かけそば一杯と同じ十六文が相場でした。しかし、「学問にはお金がかかるだろう」と言って、その倍もくださることもありました。

　こんなエピソードがあります。
　ある旗本の奥さまも、あんまが終わると、本を読んでくれるのでした。ある夏の夕暮れ、蚊帳のなかで本を読んでいた奥さまは、外でじっと聞き入っている保己一が両手を紐でゆわえているのに気づき、ふしぎそうに、聞きました。

　「その手はどうしたのですか？　蚊を追いはらうおまじないですか？」

　「いいえ、せっかく奥さまに読んでいただいているのに、蚊に気が散り、聞き逃すことがあったら大変です。蚊にまどわされないように、手をゆわえているのです」

　保己一の真剣さに、よほど感心したのでしょう。なんと平安貴族の生活を描いた『栄華物語』四十巻をくださったのです。

　印刷技術の発達していない時代、本は高価なものでしたから、お金のない保己一が〝自分の本〟を持つのはこれがはじめてで、大きな励みとなりました。

「どんなときでも希望をすててはダメよ。〝一寸先は光〟といいますからね」と口癖のように話していた母親を思いだすのでした。

両手をひもでゆわえ、蚊帳の外で聞き入る保己一。

ここにも支援者が

保己一が住む盲人一座の隣りに松平乗尹という学問に熱心な旗本が住んでいました。ある日、お師匠さまは保己一を部屋に呼んで、

「隣の松平のお殿さまが、お前が風呂敷包みを背負って歩いているのを見かけて、『あの者は何をしているのか』とおたずねになられた。『学問で身を立てたいと、あんまに出かけるときも、必ず本を持ち歩いては、親切な方に読んでいただいているのです』と話すと、『それほど書物が好きなら、わたしも読んであげてもよいが……』と言っていただいたが……」

「ぜひとも……、こんなうれしいことはありません」

こうして、一日おきに、隣のお屋敷に出かけて行き、朝のまだ暗いうちから、出仕前の半時（現在の1時間）ほど、本を読んでいただくことになりました。

＊

「保己一さんといいましたかな。どんな書物を読んでほしいのですか？」

「興味があるのは歴史物語です。学問をするのに日本の歴史に暗くてはいけないと思いまして……」

「ところで、学問はだれから学んだのですか？」

「はい、故郷の寺の和尚さまと父からです」

「これまでにどんな本を読みましたか？」

「寺子屋で和尚さまに読んでいただいた本だけです。ですから、もっともっと学びたいのです。『太平記』は和尚さまに読んでいただいたところはすべて覚えました。いつか全四十巻をすべて暗記したいと思っています」

「ほほう、全巻を！　口調はいい物語だが、覚えるのは容易ではないぞ。だが挑戦してみるのもよかろう」

右手に杖をつき、本を風呂敷につつんで背負って歩く保己一。そんな保己一に、興味ある書物を読み聞かせる旗本の殿さま。

隣のお屋敷に通い始めてしばらくして、ある日のこと、

「萩原宗固という先生を月に一度この屋敷にお呼びして、『源氏物語』や和歌の講義をしていただいている。宗固先生は日本の古典を研究している江戸でも指折りの学者です。良い機会なので、保己一さんもいっしょに講義を受けてみては……」

「はっ、はい！　ありがたいことです。ぜひとも……。」

こうして、保己一は宗固先生の講義を受けることになりました。

間もなく保己一の才能と学問への情熱に感心した乗尹さまのすすめで、宗固先生の門下生として、直接指導を受けることになったのです。

＊

それから８年、先生は新しい道をすすめてくれました。

「教えられることはすべて伝えた。学者として大成するには、わたしのところにとどまらずに、古典の研究では右に出る者がいない賀茂真淵先生のもとで、さらに学問に励むのがよかろう」

そして、真淵先生の塾に入門したのです。しかし、残念なことに、わずか半年後、先生は亡くなってしまいました。

保己一が教えを受けたのは、ほんのわずかなあいだでしたが、その後の学問と生き方に大きく影響したのです。その教えは「ものごとを判断するのには、著名な学者であるとか、世間の評判とかではなく、自分自身でよく考え、自分で判断しなければ学問は大成しない」というものでした。そのころの学問は師匠の説をそのまま無批判に受け入れる傾向があったからです。

保己一は、ほかの学者の意見を大切にしつつもそれに惑わされず、自分の〝心の目（心眼）*1〟で見て判断しました。そうした保己一の姿勢は『群書類従』*2の編集や和学講談所*3の運営など、すべての場面でつらぬかれています。

*1 塙保己一の葬儀は、大名格で行われ、その戒名は「和学院殿心眼智光大居士」。たとえ〝肉体の目〟が見えなくても〝心の目（心眼）〟で、他の学者が気づかないより深い真理に触れることができたという意味。保己一の学問のいたるところに、この真偽・善悪を見きわめる〝眼力〟が発揮されている。ヘレン・ケラーも、保己一と同じように〝心の目〟でより深く真理に触れることができたひとりである。

*2 古代から、江戸時代の初めまで1000年以上にわたり、多くの人たちが書き残した1273種類の貴重な文献や書物を法律、政治、経済、文学など25のジャンルに分類し、530巻666冊に仕立てた大文献集。すべて保己一の責任のもとで、企画、編集、校正、出版、販売がなされた。今日でも、国の内外において日本の文化を研究するためには、欠かせない生きた史料であるといわれている。

*3 1793（寛政5）年に幕府の支援を受けて保己一が創立した和学（国学）の研究・教育機関。保己一はここで多くの門弟を育てるとともに、『群書類従』『史料』をはじめ数々の歴史資料などの編集・校正を行った。

賀茂真淵先生の塾で教えを受ける保己一。

今に生きる塙保己一とヘレン・ケラー

障害者にかぎらず、すべての人が〝人間らしく〟生きられるためには、戦争のない平和な世界を実現しなければ……というのがヘレン・ケラーの信念でした。

しかし、地球上のどこかで、多くの人が傷つけあい、命を奪いあい、家族や友人が涙を流す光景が毎日のように報道されています。

今からおよそ90年も昔、平均寿命が50歳前後といわれた時代です。重度の障害をかかえた57歳のヘレンが、15日間もかけてはるばる太平洋を船で日本にわたってきた目的は「世界中の人たちに、もっと障害者を理解し、障害者に胸をはって生きてほしい」、「日本はどんなことがあっても、中国との戦争だけは避けなければならない！」と訴えるためでした。

不幸なことに、ヘレンの日本滞在中に日中戦争*がはじまり、ヘレンは途中で帰国しなければなり

ませんでした。この戦争は、差別で障害者を苦しめただけでなく、さらに多くの障害者を生み、死傷者を出したのです。

帰国したヘレンがアメリカ国内で戦争反対の声をあげると、それまで熱心に支援していた人たちも、手の平をかえすようにヘレンに「非国民！」という非難の声を浴びせたのです。そして離れていき、支援金もとだえました。

サリバン先生との二人の生活費にも困るようになったヘレンですが、平和を守るという「大きな目標を達成するためには、小さなことにこだわっていてはいけない」と自らに言い聞かせて、派手なテント小屋のショー（見世物）のステージに自ら立ちました。

生活費を稼ぐために、目も、耳も、話すのも不自由なヘレンが、自分の手で〝文字〟を書き、自分の口で〝ことば〟をしゃべり、平

平和を象徴する鳩をイメージするヘレン・ケラーと、彼女の肩をそっと抱くサリバン先生の後ろ姿。

和への思いを観客に訴えつづけたのです。"卑下することも、おごることもせず、ありのままに" 笑顔で振る舞うヘレンの姿に観客は拍手を送りました。

33

　一方、塙保己一はどうでしょうか？

　最晩年に描かれたという肖像画が温故学会の塙保己一史料館にあります。その76年の生涯は波乱に富んだものでした。幕府のおかかえ絵師の住吉広定が和学講談所に通いつめ、長女とせの助言を受けながら完成した肖像で、〝世のため、後のため〟にすべてをささげつくし、満たされた塙保己一の

ありのままの姿が、その表情ににじみでている肖像画の名作です。

　保己一の生涯は『群書類従』の編集や和学講談所の運営などで、多忙をきわめていました。しかし、〝猫の手も借りたい〟忙しいときでも、社会の一員としての盲人の尊厳をまもるために、汗をながした保己一の姿はあまり知られていません。

　老中松平定信による寛政の改革

和学講談所の講義のようす。受講者は、身分、障害の有無、年齢、貧富などを問わない。

の一環として設けられた「座中取締役」に任命された保己一は、乱れていた盲人社会の改革をすすめたのです。さらに、関東の盲人をたばねる「関東総録職」、つづいて全国の盲人社会を取りまとめる盲人一座の最高幹部「十老」の働きです。この10名の中の最高位が〝総検校〟*というわけです。総検校の期間をあわせると、足掛け29年にもなります。

特に総録職は住居を自宅を兼ねた和学講談所から本所一ッ目の総録屋敷に移しての役目でしたから、交通手段の発達していない時代、和学講談所の務めとの両立は大変だったにちがいありません。

＊当道座には厳格な階級制度がある。入門すると、まずは「初心」に、さらに73段階の位があり、最高位が「検校」。その検校の上位10人が「十老」、その最高位が「総検校」。

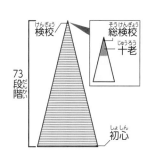

文政4（1821）年2月、満で75歳のときに総検校となった保己一。

『群書類従』等の編集・出版だけで手一杯であることを理由に、いずれの役目も辞退できたでしょう。しかし、ライフワークである学問にあてる時間を割いてまで、あえて盲人社会の重い責任を引き受けたのは、なぜでしょうか？

その背景には、幕府の盲人保護政策、なかでも特に盲人だけに認められた高利の「座頭金（金貸し）」の制度がありました。

検校のなかには、これ幸いと、あくどい手口で商売をする者もいて、盲人全体が金銭に異常なこだわりを見せる "守銭奴" でもあるかのように、軽蔑の目で見られたのです。

＊

江戸でこんな事件が評判になりました。ある旗本が急にお金が必要となり、座頭金はこわいと知りながら、やむをえず借金をしました。返済期日に返せず、厳しい取り立てに耐えきれずに夜逃げをしたのです。その結果、お家は取り

つぶしに……。一方、検校たちは不当に高い金利と強引な取り立てを理由に、財産没収のうえ江戸から追放されたのです。

「夜逃げの貧乏旗本に贅沢三昧の金持検校」と陰口をたたかれるほど、一部の検校の思いあがった行動が世間の批判を浴び、これが盲人全体への差別の原因にもなっていました。

保己一にとって、盲人一座とのかかわりは大きな負担になりましたが、亡くなるまで、その関係を大切にしました。盲目という運命をせおう仲間が互いに助け合うという盲人一座の伝統を守るとともに、その道を外れるようなことがあれば、どんなに忙しくても、解決のために汗をながしたのです。

盲人の社会的地位向上のためには一座の高い役職についていなければ、なんの改革もできないことに気づいた保己一が、すべて "世のため、後のため" * を考えてのことでした。

＊「世のため、後のため」は保己一のキャッチフレーズ。出世や蓄財に淡白だった保己一は、金がなければ出世がむずかしい盲人社会で、最高位の「総検校」にまで出世した。しかし、妬む声が聞こえてこないのは、『世のため、後のため』に身を削って活動する保己一の誠実な生き方にあった。その姿を目にした人たちは身分や立場をこえて、その活動を物心両面から支援した。

盲目の身で日本古来の文化を後世に伝えた塙保己一は、盲人にとってあこがれの存在であり、すべての人にとっても人生の目標となる先人でもある。世のため、後のために生涯をささげた保己一を仰ぎ見る若い盲人たち。

おわりに（未来へ希望をつなぐ）

塙保己一を人生の目標としたというヘレン・ケラーですが、自分の生涯をふりかえり、次のように言っています。

「わたしは、すすむべき道に迷ったときには、よく林に出かけました。そんな木々の間を歩いていると、いつも、暗い土の中で、元気にがんばっている根がうたう歌が聞こえてくるのです。〝木々の根〟は、自分ががんばって咲かせた美しい花を、自分では見ることができないのですが、決して不平を言わないのです」（ヘレン・ケラー『私の宗教』）

ヘレンは人々の〝幸せ〟を支える〝根〟の役割を演じて生涯を終えました。ときには「三重苦の聖女」とたたえられ、ときには戦争反対を唱える「非国民」と激しい非難を浴びせられましたが、「すべての人に幸せを！」という信念は少しもゆらぐことはありませんでした。

それでは、保己一はどうでしょうか？

国学の四大人（四大国学者）として、荷田春満、賀茂真淵、本居宣長、平田篤胤があげられますが、〝国学者・塙保己一〟の名はありません。

保己一は、この表舞台で活躍した四人の学者とは対照的な道をえらびました。学問の基礎となる正確な歴史資料を提供することに全人生をささげ、多くの学者たちの研究を土台から支えたのです。学問全体の発展のためには、だれかがこの役割をはたさなければならないと考えたからです。

旗本と同等ともいわれた〝検校さま〟といえば、金をためこみ、権威の象徴である紫色の豪華な衣と派手なかぶり物で身をよそおい、背の高さほどもある検校杖を手に、供を連れて街にくりだしていたのです。そんな姿を見なれて

たがいに向かい合う、ヘレン・ケラーと塙保己一。二人の偉人に光が注がれている。

いた人たちは、いつも木綿の普段着姿の保己一が本を風呂敷にくるんで背に負い、杖をたよりに街なかを訪ね歩く姿に、親しみと敬意を覚えたにちがいありません。

ここでも、日本とアメリカの二人の偉人のあいだには、どんなときでも〝卑下せず、おごらず、ありのままに生きる〟という共通した姿が見えてきます。

21世紀は「共生の100年」「福祉の世紀」といわれますが、今こそ、〝世のため、後のため〟を目標に、未来をも見通して訴えつづけた塙保己一とヘレン・ケラーの二人の偉人に、もう一度目を向けてみてはいかがでしょうか？

心身に障害のある人たちは、常に社会の少数者です。同じ社会の一員として、〝誰ひとり取り残さない社会の実現〟は、21世紀に生きる私たち一人ひとりの願いであり、責任です。塙保己一とヘレン・ケラーの願いは、そのまま今日のSDGs（持続可能な開発目標）＊の時代に生きる私たちへのメッセージではないでしょうか。

＊今のままでは、地球は立ちゆかないほど危機的な状態にある。日本政府は「（SDGsとは）持続可能でよりよい世界を目指す国際目標です。17のゴール・169のターゲットから構成され、地球上の誰一人取り残さないことを誓っています。SDGsは発展途上国のみならず、先進国自身が取り組むユニバーサル（普遍的）なものであり、日本としても積極的に取り組んでいます」と発表している。

読者のみなさまへ

　本書は、今から277年前の江戸時代に、現在の埼玉県本庄市児玉町で誕生した視覚障害のある偉人「塙 保己一」の一生をもとにつくられた絵本です。

　保己一は、国学者として大成し、さらに盲人社会の最高位である総検校まで昇り詰めた人です。幾多の困難にも負けずに、学問の基礎となる歴史資料を提供することに全人生を捧げました。

　保己一の生きざまにはすべて「世のため、後のため」の理念があり、その理念を未来に向けて訴え続けました。生涯にわたり「群書類従の編集」「和学講談所の運営」に携わり、人格者である保己一の周りには多くの人たちが集い、身分や立場を超えてその活動を支援しました。

　保己一は14歳で江戸へ出て雨富検校のもとであん摩・鍼治療を学ぶのですが、生来手先が不器用なために学問の道で身を立てる決心をし、雨富検校もその意志の強さに打たれ面倒を見てくれたのでした。周りのさまざまな人に書物を読んでもらって知識を増やし、高名な講義を聞いて心の眼（心眼）を養い、不断の努力により『群書類従』の編集に至ります。

　エピソードとして残っているものの一つにこのような話があります。ある夏の夜のこと、和学講談所で「源氏物語」の講義の最中に風が吹いてろうそくの火が消えてしまったことがありました。保己一はそれとは知らずに講義を続け、晴眼の弟子たちが暗闇であわてたところ、「目が見える人は不自由なものですね」と一言。これを聞いて、弟子たちはどっと笑ったのでした。心の眼で、ものの本質を見抜くことの大切さを伝えようとした、忘れられない逸話です。視覚と聴覚の障害を持つヘレン・ケラー（1880年－1968年）もこのエピソードを良く知っていて、感銘を受けたことを訪日の折の講演会で話していました。

　ヘレン・ケラーは幼少のときから「保己一を手本にしなさい」と母親に教育をされていました。ヘレンが1937（昭和12）年に東京の渋谷にある「温故学会」を訪れた際、保己一の座像や机に触れる機会があり、挫折しそうになった自分は、先生を思いだしては立ち直ることが出来たと述べられています。さらには、「先生のお名前は流れる水のように永遠に伝わるでしょう」とも語っておられました。二人の間には「卑下せず、おごらず、ありのままに生きるという共通の姿が見えています」と本文中でも言及しています。

　絵本の作成は、文では堺正一氏の巧みな文体により、塙保己一のこと、ヘレン・ケラーとの繋がりが良くわかるようにまとめていただきました。絵は吉澤みかさんに江戸期の情景を美しく表現してもらいました。

　本書の発行にあたり、小学館、一般財団法人日本児童教育振興財団より、ご支援を賜わりましたことに厚く御礼申し上げます。また、この絵本の製作に関わっていただいた全ての方々に、当会を代表して深く御礼申し上げます。

2023年12月
社会福祉法人　桜雲会　理事長　一幡良利

文／堺正一

1943年、埼玉県生まれ。早稲田大学法学部・同教育学部卒業。埼玉県立盲学校（現塙保己一学園）等の校長、立正大学教授等を歴任。長年、障害のある子どもの教育にたずさわり、障害児者理解推進のために、講演、著述、ボランティア活動等に取り組む。著書に『今に生きる塙保己一』（埼玉新聞社）、『塙保己一とともに　ヘレン・ケラーと塙保己一』（はる書房）など多数。第15回塙保己一賞（貢献賞）受賞。

絵／吉澤みか

1963年京都府生まれ。日本画家。京都精華大学美術学部造形学科日本画専攻卒業。京都市立芸術大学美術学部大学院修了。京都美術展（奨励賞受賞）、京展ほか入選多数。大人も読める絵本『ざっそう weeds』『駅のピアノ　故国への想い』（ともに今人舎）の絵を担当。

英訳／ノビ・キーリ（Nobby Kealey）

1957年イギリス・マンチェスター生まれ。シェフィールド大学にて日本語を専攻。来日後はカメラマンとして活躍する一方、英語教師のほか、数々のテレビCMに出演。松蔭学園イングリッシュ・スクール校長。

監修／社会福祉法人　桜雲会

1892年、東京盲唖学校（現在の筑波大学附属視覚特別支援学校）の生徒の同窓会として発足。1930年に最初の鍼按科教科書を出版。以後、医学専門書を中心に点字図書や録音図書、拡大図書の製作・販売をおこなう。

協力／公益社団法人 温故学会

編集・デザイン・DTP制作／
　株式会社 今人舎（二宮祐子／矢野瑛子／高橋博美）

すべて世のため、後のために 塙保己一とヘレン・ケラー

2024年2月10日 初版発行　　　　　　　　　　　　　　　　NDC289

文	堺正一
絵	吉澤みか
発行者	一幡良利
発行所	社会福祉法人桜雲会
	〒169-0075 東京都新宿区高田馬場4-11-14-102
	電話　03-5337-7866　http://ounkai.jp
印刷・製本	瞬報社写真印刷株式会社

©Shouichi Sakai, Mika Yoshizawa 2024, Printed in Japan, Published by Ounkai　　48P　210×260mm
ISBN978-4-911208-00-7

For The Sake Of All, For The Sake Of The Future
--Hanawa Hokiichi and Helen Keller

Text: Sakai Shōichi   Illustrations: Yoshizawa Mika

P2-3

Introduction (The Japanese Person Who Was A Pillar Of Spiritual Support To Helen Keller)

Many biographies of great people have been published and the biography of Helen Keller, an American woman who faced challenges with her sight, hearing and speech, is one of the most representative of these.

Helen visited Japan three times in her life. Her first visit was in Showa 12 (1937) when she was 57 years old, during a period known for the saying "a life lasts only 50 years". The severely disabled Helen travelled from San Francisco to Japan aboard a ship called the Asama Maru. Declining to rest after the long 15-day voyage, she immediately went to visit the Hanawa Hokiichi Historical Archives at the Onko Academic Society Hall in the Shibuya area of Tokyo.

She was deeply moved by this visit and went on to give a speech to a packed audience at Saitama Public Hall in Urawa. She began her speech like this:

"Every time I felt like giving up, I would think of Master Hanawa Hokiichi and find the strength to recover. That is how I have got to where I am today. I thought that, one day, I'd like to come to Japan and visit Saitama, the hometown of my role model, Master Hanawa. Today that wish has come true."

Actually, since her childhood, Helen had heard about this blind Japanese scholar from her mother as she grew up. Her mother always told her this:

"In Japan, there was a teacher named Hanawa Hokiichi who worked hard and became a great scholar, despite losing his eyesight at a young age. During his time, there was no Braille nor schools for the blind and the only way for him to learn was to have books read to him and to memorize them. But you are different. We now have Braille that lets you read and write by yourself, and there are schools for the deaf and blind. Plus, isn't your private tutor, Miss Sullivan, always there by your side providing guidance? So, even when things get tough, think of Master Hanawa and always do your best."

*

During the Meiji era, this young girl's story also spread to the Japanese education sector. It became a topic of great interest, with people saying the following had been proved to be true: "No matter how severe a child's disabilities, as long as the opportunity for an education is guaranteed, that child can grow into a fine human being."

So, what kind of person was this Japanese scholar who Helen Keller had made her role model and who was to provide her with such spiritual support?

※Hanawa Hokiichi's name changed many times during his lifetime. To avoid confusion, in this book, we will refer to him in his childhood as 'Tatsunosuke', in the period when he began his studies in Edo as 'Senya' and after he embarked on the path of scholarship as 'Hanawa Hokiichi'.

Caption:
Helen Keller speaks of her feelings towards Hanawa Hokiichi in a lecture.

P4-5

The Eye Doctor

This following relates to when Tatsunosuke (later Hanawa Hokiichi) suffered from eye problems but was still able to see. He was the first-born son of a farmer in the northern part of Musashino Province, now known as Kodama-chō, Honjō City, Saitama Prefecture.

Despite being 2 ri (about 8km) from their home, Tatsunosuke's mother would take him for treatment to an eye doctor in Fujioka Village in Kōzukeno Province (now Fujioka City, Gunma Prefecture). The doctor there, Kiribuchi Kōsuke, was renowned for treating eye ailments. He had an affinity for haikai poetry (now known as haiku) and was also a scholar with a deep love of learning.

New Year had passed and the young Tatsunosuke, led by his mother, with the view of the snow-capped Mt. Asama in the distance, finally arrived at the doctor's. Dr. Kiribuchi called out kindly to him,

"Tatsunosuke, well done! You made it all the way here despite the north wind."

As Tatsunosuke and his mother came in, their faces flushed from the cold, the doctor clasped Tatsunosuke's hands in his own warm hands, then asked him,

"Tatsunosuke, what is your favorite food?"

"Tsumikko! It's warm and delicious."

"That's perfect. We just had some ourselves. Wouldn't you and your mother like to eat a little? It'll warm you up."

'Tsumikko' is a local dish, a kind of 'suiton', a broth containing dumplings made with locally grown wheat and lots of vegetables. In this region, where wheat cultivation and sericulture have been popular since ancient times, it was often eaten during breaks from work or in the cold season.

"Doctor, thank you for the meal. It was delicious, wasn't it, Mom?"

"It certainly was, Tatsunosuke. It's the best treat when it's cold…and now look, this child's forehead is covered in sweat!"

Caption:
    Tatsunosuke enjoys eating delicious 'tsumikko'.

P6-7

"Tatsunosuke, on your way here, what were the farmers doing in the fields?"

"They were all doing 'mugifumi' (treading wheat). I help my Mom with the treading, too. If we don't do the treading, we can't get good wheat for 'tsumikko'. Right, Mom?"

"Do you know why we do wheat treading, Tatsunosuke?"

"They say that if we don't tread the wheat, it won't become strong enough to withstand the cold. Treading makes it strong against the frost and north winds."

"I can see you understand it well. Treading on the young wheat may seem cruel, but if that isn't done, it won't bear good grains. That's why they tread it 3 or 4 times while it is young. Humans are the same…..we may face hardships and feel trodden on many times, but we mustn't forget that each time makes us stronger. Just because it's cold, sitting around the hearth all the time won't make you a strong child."

"Doctor, I'm OK. After all, 'a child is a child of the wind'."

"…Mother, Tatsunosuke is a smart child. It's like he has an 'eye of the heart'…. there are 'important things that are noticed because one can't see', I guess."

From that day forward, Tatsunosuke never forgot the doctor's words, "Every hardship makes you that much tougher". Despite the bitter cold winds, he continued to help with the wheat treading.

However, despite his visits to the doctor when he was around 5 years old, Tatsunosuke's vision deteriorated to the point where he could barely see at all.

When Tatsunosuke's parents were told by the doctor that he would never see again, they were at a loss and were worried for his future.

Caption:
    Tatsunosuke happily treads wheat alongside his mother.

P8-9

His Tutor the Buddhist Monk

As usual, the lively voices of children could be heard coming from the temple school of Ryusei Temple, which was located behind Tatsunosuke's house.

Tatsunosuke's mother, who was watching her son absentmindedly lounging in the sun on the veranda, said, "Tatsunosuke must also want to learn something*….. It's such a shame it brings tears to my eyes. Couldn't we ask the monk to help him, dear?"

"I understand how you feel, mother….but, as he can't see, I'm sure it would only be causing trouble for the monk….. It's a pity for Tatsunosuke, but….."

*

One day, leaning on his cane, Tatsunosuke made his way to the shade of a nutmeg tree at Ryusei Temple and quietly observed the activities of the temple school. Noticing him there, the monk called out to him,

"Tatsunosuke, why don't you come over here and learn with us?"

In the Edo era, education at a temple school consisted of learning to read and write characters and calligraphy.

Caption:
    The monk calls out softly to Tatsunosuke, who is observing the temple school from the shade of a nutmeg tree.

P10-11

"…Reverend, Tatsu-chan can't see, so isn't it impossible for him to learn?"

"You shouldn't say such things. Come on, Tatsunosuke, come over here."

Using his cane, Tatsunosuke hesitatingly made his way in. Looking down, he said,

"But…, I can't see….."

"Don't worry about that. Hurry up and come here. From now on this will be Tatsunosuke's seat. Now, listen everyone, starting tomorrow, be sure to guide Tatsunosuke to this spot."

The monk thought that even just being with a group of friends would be better for Tatsunosuke than idling away his days at home on his own.

And so, with a designated seat in the corner of the temple's main hall, Tatsunosuke listened intently to the lessons.

The monk was worried that he might not be able to keep up with the others, but Tatsunosuke came every day with a bright smile on his face. Seeing how he had regained his enthusiasm, Tatsunosuke's parents were extremely grateful to the monk.

Caption:
    (P10)Guided by the monk, Tatsunosuke takes his seat at the temple school. A bright smile lights up his face.

(P11)His parents are pleased to see Tatsunosuke's smiling face. Their hearts are filled with gratitude to the monk.

P12-13

One day, the monk told the children a story about a 'biwa hōshi'. A biwa hōshi was a blind entertainer who dressed as a Buddhist monk and recited the 'Heikemonogatari' ('The Tale of Heike') *1 while playing the biwa, a stringed instrument. The children were overjoyed when the monk raised his voice on high and performed passionately, just like an actual biwa hōshi.

"The sound of the Gion Shōja bells
Echoes the impermanence of all things.
The color of the sala flowers
Reveals the truth that the prosperous must decline."

....

Tatsunosuke was captivated by the passage that said, "The arrogant Heike Clan shall not be around for long." Noticing how intently Tatsunosuke listened, the monk could see his keen interest in historical tales and he began to find time to read to him little by little from 'The Taiheiki' ('The Tale of Great Peace')*2, which was popular in Edo at that time.

Surprisingly, Tatsunosuke was able to completely remember even difficult tales containing classical Chinese texts. Then, he would go back home and retell the stories in front of his parents and elderly neighbors, closely imitating the monk's voice as he spoke, thus becoming renowned among the villagers for his story-telling skills.

However, Tatsunosuke wasn't always accepted into the group of children. Maybe his ability to excel at learning, despite his blindness, was the cause of some unkindness towards him. Perhaps this led him to direct his interests even more towards academic studies.

"History is so fascinating. The 'Taiheiki' that the monk reads to us apparently has 40 volumes, but, someday, I want to remember it all. If a blind biwa hōshi can memorize the whole of 'The Tale of Heike', there is no reason I can't do it!", he thought.

And so, the tiny seed of learning planted in the young boy's heart with the help of the monk sprouted and, despite facing hardships and challenges, like a field of wheat exposed to the wind and rain, it grew strong and resilient.

*1 Written during the Kamakura era for blind 'biwa hōshi' to narrate, this is a tale depicting the rise and fall of the Heike Clan.
*2 This is a tale depicting battles over more than 50 years, from the end of the Kamakura era to the Nanboku-chō era. It became very popular during the Edo era, taking the place of the 'Heikemonogatari' recited by 'biwa hōshi', thanks to the performances of entertainers known as 'Taiheiki Yomi'.

Caption:
    A picture of a blind biwa hōshi. They mainly recited military stories, such as 'The Tale of Heike', while playing the biwa, a stringed instrument.

P14-15

Longing To Go To Edo And Setbacks

In the summer of Tatsunosuke's 11th year, his mother fell seriously ill due to complications of a cold and, despite the family's desperate efforts, she sadly passed away. It was a sudden loss and Tatsunosuke blamed himself, thinking that her death might have been a result of the hardships she suffered from her efforts to take care of him. While he was feeling devastated at the loss of the mother who had loved him so, a silk merchant who visited every year to buy silkworm cocoons told him the following:
"In the past, when people talked about blind performers, they usually referred to the 'Heike Biwa', but these days, the figure of the 'biwa hōshi' is rarely seen in Edo. Instead, the 'Taiheiki Yomi', who recites the 'Taiheiki' in front of audiences, has become very popular and performance spaces have sprung up here and there that are always filled with customers. I had a chance to hear you reciting the 'Taiheiki' and it was really magnificent. Unlike a 'biwa hōshi', I've never heard a 'Taiheiki Yomi' before, but if it's Tatsunosuke, with proper training, I'm sure he can excel at it."
When he heard these words, Tatsunosuke's heart leapt with excitement and he could barely stand still.
"The 'Taiheiki' that the monk read to me....I wanted to memorize all of it....there's no other job better suited to me...."
In his mind, Tatsunosuke imagined himself in Edo, reciting the 'Taiheiki'.

*

Worried about his blind son venturing alone into Edo where he knew nobody, his father was opposed to the idea. However, Tatsunosuke's determined pleas eventually persuaded him, and thinking, "If this was to open a new path to my son's future.....", he allowed him to go.
And so, in the summer of his 14th year, guided by the hand of that silk merchant, Tatsunosuke set out on his journey to Edo.

Caption:
    A rear view of Tatsunosuke setting out for Edo, carrying a change of clothes and other items in a wooden box (later called 'the treasure box') in a wrapping cloth.

P16-17

In Edo, Tatsunosuke found refuge in a guild of blind people* lead by the renowned acupuncturist Ametomi Sugaichi Kengyō. Upon entering the guild, according to their custom, he shaved his head and changed his name to Senya, marking the beginning of his new life. However, life in Edo was not as easy as he had imagined.

At that time, the shogunate recognized special rights for blind people in certain professions, including entertainment such as shamisen and koto playing, anma massage therapy, acupuncture and, additionally, privileges as money lenders, know as 'zatō-gane'.

However, unlike the other apprentices, Senya had come to Edo with the faint hope of becoming a Taiheiki Yomi, believing that this could lead him on the path to academic studies, so he lacked the drive to practice the shamisen or anma massage, in which he had no interest at all.

Without motivation, improvement was impossible. He was criticized by the other apprentices as a 'lazy person', and eventually, he was labelled a 'freeloader'. Senya felt he had no place in the guild.

*During that time, blind people had set up a self-governing organization officially recognized by the shogunate called 'Tōdōza' which provided vocational training in anma massage skills, acupuncture, moxibustion, the koto, the shamisen or the biwa. At the same time, it was also a community in which members helped and supported each other in their daily lives.

Caption:
    Changing his name to Senya, he undergoes training in anma massage and the shamisen. However, his face shows his disappointment in himself for not putting in any effort at all.

On top of that, this child developed a fever and we had to pay the doctor for medicine. Can I ask you to wait until next month…..?"

In the end, he was unable to collect the debt that day and he was accused of being "useless!" by his senior apprentice. Knowing that, without their tools, craftsmen could not go to work or support their families, the lenders would forcefully demand their loans be repaid, even using such threats as, "We will hold on to your toolbox until you pay your debts!" On top of the high interest rates, such collection methods meant they were much feared by the general public.*

Senya, however, couldn't bring himself to follow such practices.

"If things continue like this, I'll never be able to pursue my studies. But if I was to run back to my hometown, I wouldn't be able to face the villagers who saw me off on my trip. Perhaps it would be better if I was to join my late mother…."

*In the blind community (Tōdōza) there were intricate hierarchies which had originally been based on a person's skill and reputation. However, by Senya's time, all these positions could be bought with money. But modest earnings from such things as massage fees made gaining promotions very difficult. Therefore, the shogunate allowed for very high interest rates to be charged when lending that money to specifically protect blind people. This came to be known as 'zatō-gane'. As a result, many blind people abandoned their traditional livelihoods in pursuit of profit-making, becoming a problem in society.

Caption:
    Senya is in despair after being blamed by a senior apprentice for failing to collect a debt.

P18-19

The Blind and Money Lending (Zatō-Gane)

One day, Senya was assigned the task of collecting a debt by one of his senior apprentices.

"There's a carpenter named Yahei in a tenement house in the Mikawa-chō area of Kanda.

We lent him 1ryō and 2 bu of money and today is the day for him to pay back the interest, so go and collect it."

"….Ye…Yes, sir,…I understand", Senya responded hesitantly, but he had a kind heart and a task like collecting a debt was impossible for him.

Senya reluctantly set out, but his fears were justified. The carpenter's wife apologized, explaining that she had borrowed the money for necessities like food, but now she didn't have the money to pay it back.

"My husband caught a bad cold and couldn't go to work.

P20-21

The Drawstring Bag of Love and The Master of the Guild

One afternoon, upon seeing the other apprentices leave, Senya quietly slipped out of the residence. He wandered aimlessly, relying on his cane, but when he came to Ushigafuchi, one of the moats around Edo Castle, he slipped and fell into the water. While he was struggling, his hand touched the drawstring bag that was a memento of his mother and which he always kept close to his body. At that time, his mother's voice echoed clearly in his ears:

"You mustn't die like this! I don't remember raising such a weakling. No matter how difficult it is, you must live! Didn't I teach you, 'the light is just a short step ahead'*? You will live!"

Suddenly, he was aware of someone calling his name.

"Senya, grab this sash…hold on tightly!"

*'*What's ahead is darkness' is an idiom that means, 'you never know what's going to happen just a little further down the road'. There isn't an idiom that says, 'The light is just a short step ahead'. Probably trying to allay her blind son's fears a little, Senya's mother likely changed 'darkness' to the more hopeful 'light' when she spoke to him.*

Caption:
As Senya struggles on the surface of the moat with a drawstring bag in his hand, an image of his mother comes to his mind.

P22-23

The person who had taken off his own sash and thrown it down to Senya to rescue him was an elderly servant at the residence of Ametomi Kengyō named Wasuke.
He quickly returned with Senya to the residence and upon entering he called out,
"Master Kengyō, Master Kengyō!"
"…What is it, Wasuke? Calm down…"
"I can't calm down. It's Senya… It's lucky I was passing by, it was almost a disaster. At Ushigafuchi…."
"What…. Senya threw himself in?"

*

After changing into dry clothes, Senya sat dejectedly beside Wasuke in front of Ametomi Kengyō.
"Wasuke, tell me what happened."
"…Well, I was on my way back from some errands and, as I approached Ushigafuchi, I felt the presence of a someone…. A sense of foreboding told me something was wrong. Normally, I would have just kept going, but something felt strange and I turned back. To my surprise, I saw a man struggling in the moat. In a frenzy, I untied my waist sash and threw it down to him."
"Senya, I was just worrying about what's been going on with you lately."
"…….."
"Why would you think of killing yourself? Please, tell me everything."
"A year ago, I persuaded my father, who was against it, to allow me to come here to Edo and become one of your apprentices. I'd heard that, in Edo, even a blind person could live a full life if you made an effort…. But…..I'm just no good at anything. I have no interest in anma massage or the shamisen. But I can't go back to the countryside now and I was thinking it would be easier to go to be with my dead mother…before I knew it, I was by the moat. After that, I just….."
"What is this? I was always planning to have a talk with you, but…. Now, you just said you wanted to die. Do you think your late mother would be happy to hear that? I'm sure your father would feel the same way…."
"Master….."
"Anyway, what exactly is it that you want to do? The koto, the shamisen, anma massage, acupuncture, these are the vocations given to us blind people. Everyone finds what is suitable for them and makes a living. Yet, you…."
"Everyone, I….."

Caption:
After being rescued by Wasuke and returned to the mansion, Ametomi Kengyō listens to Senya's story.

P24-25

"But you aren't a bad person. Since I first met you, I've believed that, if you had determination, you could do more than the average person…and I still think that. But I don't see that determination in you. Tell me what it is you want to do."
"….Well, I want to be a reader of the 'Taiheiki', and if possible, pursue scholarly studies…."
"What, what did you say? Speak up, speak clearly!"
"….When I'm doing anma massage training, I can't get the thought of being a scholar out of my head. …..Back home, the monk at a nearby temple read me 'The Tale of the Heike' and 'The Taiheiki'. To me, there is nothing more fascinating than this."
"But, a blind man who can't read or write can't possibly make a living from academic study, no matter how much he likes it."
"I understand it is difficult, but I'm willing to undergo any hardships for the sake of my studies."
"Until now, I never saw anything in you, Senya, that said to me, "Ah, this is it…." However, one time, when I was teaching from Sugiyama Kengyō's medical text, I was impressed with your powers of understanding, memorization and concentration. …….If you truly want to pursue these scholarly studies and are prepared for the difficulties ahead, I think you should try your hardest to do what you want to do. I will take care of your living expenses…..But, if I can't see any progress after 3 years, I'll send you back to your home in Kodama, that'll be the end of it."
"….Oh, thank you. Even though, by all rights I should be expelled, you are willing to let me pursue the thing I desire. From now on, I'll try my hardest, even at anma massage training."
"OK, OK, there's no need for tears. Just don't ever entertain such strange thoughts again. Try not to do anything that would sadden your late mother or your father back at home in the village."

Caption:
  Two images associated with Senya's aspirations to become
  a scholar. One is an academic text book, the other is a
  keepsake of his mother, a handmade cotton drawstring
  purse. It was made as a kind of lucky charm by reusing an
  old obi sash, and Hokiichi carried it close to him all his life.

P26-27

Supported By Volunteer Readers

Hokiichi, having changed his name from Senya,
immediately began pursuing his scholarly studies. Before
long, rumors such as the following began to spread:
"I've heard there is a young apprentice of Ametomi
Kengyō who carries books with him wherever he goes
and when he has finished performing anma massage, he
asks to be read to, even if they can only spare a very short
time for him."
With no money, Hokiichi had nothing to offer in return
except his massage skills. Therefore, he dedicated himself
fully to his training. He improved to the point where he
became known as 'Hokiichi the anma expert', his
reputation grew and the number of his supporters increased.
At that time, the usual price of an anma massage was
about 16 mon, the equivalent of a bowl of soba noodles in
soup. However, knowing the cost of academic studies,
there were times when some generous people willingly
paid double that amount.
Then, there was also this episode. The wife of a certain
'hatamoto' (a high ranking samurai in service to the
Tokugawa shogunate) would read to Hokiichi after one of
his anma massages. One summer evening, as she read
from a book inside the mosquito net and Hokiichi sat
outside listening intently, she noticed that his hands were
clasped together, bound with string. She was curious and
asked him,
 "Why are your hands like that? Is it a charm to drive away
the mosquitoes?"
"No. It would be terrible if I was to miss something
because I was distracted by mosquitoes while Madam was
so kindly reading to me. My hands are like this so I am not
led astray by the mosquitoes."
Impressed by his sincerity, she made a gift to him of a
copy of the 40-volume 'Eigamonogatari' ('The Tale of
Glory'), a story depicting aristocratic life in the Heian
period.
In a time when printing technology was not yet advanced,
books were expensive items and, having no money, this
was the first time Hokiichi had owned a book of his own
and it served as a great encouragement for him.
He recalled what his mother had so often repeated, "Never
give up hope, because, as they say, 'the light is just a short

step ahead'".

Caption:
  With both hands bound by string, Hokiichi listens intently
  from outside the mosquito net as a book is read to him.

P28-29

Here's Another Supporter

Residing in the mansion next door to the blind people's
guild where Hokiichi lived was a hatamoto named
Matsudaira Noritada who was also a keen scholar. One
day, Hokiichi's master called him into his room and said,
"The neighboring Lord Matsudaira has noticed you
carrying a wrapped bundle on your back when you go out
and asked, "What is that man doing?" I told him, "He
wants to make a name for himself as a scholar and so,
even when he goes out to perform anma massage, he
always carries a book with him in the hope that a kind
person will read to him" to which he replied, "Well, if he
loves books that much, I could read to him....""
"Yes, by all means! Nothing would make me happier."
So, every other day he would go to the neighboring
mansion early in the morning while it was still dark and
for about one hour, before his duties began, Lord
Matsudaira would read to him.

*

"Did you say your name was Hokiichi? Now, what kind of
book would you like me to read?"
"I'm interested in historical tales. I think it's essential for
my studies that I know about Japanese history...."
"By the way, from whom did you receive your learning?"
"From a monk in a temple in my hometown and from my
father."
"Which books have you read so far?"
"Only the books that the monk in the temple school read
to me. That's why I want to learn more. I've memorized
all the parts of 'The Taiheiki' that the monk read to me.
Someday, I want to memorize all 40 volumes."
"Oh my! All the volumes! It's a story of great courage and
bravery, but that won't be an easy task. However, I think
it would be good to take on such a challenge."

Caption:
  Hokiichi walks with his cane in his right hand and carries
  books in a wrapping cloth on his back. The feudal lord reads
  from a book of interest to Hokiichi.

One day, sometime after he began visiting the neighboring mansion, they had the following conversation:

"Once a month, I invite a teacher named Hagiwara Sōko to this mansion to give lectures on 'Genjimonogatari' ('The Tale of Genji') and waka poetry. Master Sōko is considered one of the leading scholars in Edo in the study of Japanese Classics. It's a great opportunity, so how about joining us at the lectures, Hokiichi?"

"Yes, yes! Thank you so much. Of course...."

And so he began attending Master Sōko's lectures at the mansion. Before long, at the recommendation of Lord Matsudaira, who had been so impressed by his talent and passion for learning, Hokiichi became a disciple of Master Sōko and began receiving direct instruction.

*

After 8 years had passed, his teacher recommended a different path for Hokiichi.

"I've taught you everything I can. In order to excel as a scholar, it is better that you don't stay here with me, but it would be good for you to further your studies under Master Kamo no Mabuchi, who is unmatched in the study of the classics."

So, Hokiichi enrolled in Master Mabuchi's private academy. Unfortunately, however, just 6 months later, the teacher passed away. Although Hokiichi's time studying under Mabuchi was brief, it greatly influenced his subsequent academic pursuits and way of life.

His core teaching was, "To judge matters, rely not on the ideas of famous scholars or public opinion, but think critically for yourself. Without this ability to decide things for yourself, great scholarship cannot be achieved." This was important because,in those days, academics tended to uncritically accept their master's theories as they were.

While respecting the opinions of other scholars, Hokiichi was not swayed by them and made judgements based on what he saw with his own 'mind's eye'*1, a stance he maintained throughout various endeavors, such as editing the 'Gunsho Ruijū' ('The Great Collection of Old Documents')*2 and managing the Wagaku Kōdansho Institute*3 and which became a hallmark of his approach to every situation.

*1 When Hokiichi passed away, a funeral befitting a person of the Daimyo rank was held for him and his posthumous name was given as 'Wagakuinden-shingan-chikō-daikoji', (roughly meaning 'Venerable Devotee and Master of National Studies Illuminated by the Light of the Mind's Eye'). This signified that, even though his 'physical eyes' couldn't see, his 'heart's eye' ('mind's eye') would have allowed him to perceive deeper truths than other scholars were aware of. Hanawa Hokiichi's ability to discern between truth and falsehood, good and evil, is evident throughout his scholarly career. Helen Keller was another who, like Hokiichi, was able to access deeper truths through her 'mind's eye'.

*2 This is a large collection of 1273 valuable texts and documents written by numerous people over more than 1000 years, from ancient times to the early Edo period, classified into 25 genres, such as law, politics, economics, literature etc., and assembled into 666 books in 530 volumes. Hokiichi was responsible for the planning, editing, proofreading, printing and sales of the complete set. Even today, it is said to be an indispensable living archive for the study of Japanese culture, both within the country and abroad.

*3 A research and educational institute for the study of Wagaku (Japanese National Studies) established by Hokiichi in 1793 (Kansei 5) with the support of the shogunate. Here, he nurtured many disciples and, starting with the 'Gunsho Ruijū' and 'Shiryō', undertook the editing and proofreading of numerous historical documents.

Caption:
Hokiichi attends a lesson at the private academy of Master Kamo no Mabuchi.

The Living Legacies of Hanawa Hokiichi and Helen Keller

It was Helen Keller's belief that, for all people to live 'humanely', not just those with disabilities, a world at peace and without war must be realized. Yet, somewhere in the world, scenes of people being hurt or losing their lives and families and friends shedding tears are reported daily.

About 90 years ago it was an age when the average lifespan was said to be around 50 years. Helen, a 57-year old woman with severe disabilities, undertook a 15-day voyage across the Pacific Ocean by ship all the way to Japan, to convey her messages: "I want all the world to understand disabled people better and for disabled people to live with pride," and "War between Japan and China must be avoided at all costs!"

Unfortunately, during Helen's stay in Japan, the Sino-Japanese War* broke out and she had to return home early. This war not only caused the disabled to suffer due to discrimination, but also created more disabled people and caused many casualties.

When Helen returned to America and spoke out against the war, people who had previously been enthusiastic supporters accused her of being 'unpatriotic'. They turned away from her and her donations dried up.

Helen now found it hard to provide living expenses for her and Miss Sullivan, but she told herself, "In order to achieve such a great things as the preservation of peace, we must not be too concerned about small thing" and, with such an attitude in mind, she willingly took to

47

personally appearing on stage in a gaudy tented hut in a kind of carnival show.

To earn a living, Helen, who was blind, deaf and unable to speak, wrote 'letters' with her own hand and spoke 'words' with her own mouth to convey her message of peace to the audience. They applauded Helen, who performed with a smile on her face and was 'without condescension or arrogance, living authentically'.

The full-scale war between Japan and China that lasted from 1937 to 1945. In 1941, negotiations broke down between Japan and America over demands that Japan withdraw its troops from China, leading to war with the Allied Powers, including America, Britain and China (The Pacific War). In July 1945, the Potsdam Declaration was announced, calling for Japan's unconditional surrender. Japan accepted it in August of the same year, leading to the end of the war.

Caption:
A rear view of Helen Keller imagining a dove symbolizing peace, while Miss Sullivan gently embraces her shoulders.

P34-35

On the other hand, what of Hanawa Hokiichi? A portrait of him, said to have been painted in his final years, is held in the Hanawa Hokiichi Historical Archives at the Onko Academic Society Hall. His lifetime of 76 years was certainly eventful. Sumiyoshi Hirosada, personal painter to the shogunate, completed the painting over many visits to the Wagaku Kōdansho Institute, while being advised by Hokiichi's eldest daughter, Tose. The famous portrait depicts a fulfilled Hokiichi, who gave everything 'for the sake of all, for the sake of the future', his true self reflected in his expression.

Hokiichi's life was extremely busy with his various tasks, such as editing the 'Gunsho Ruijū' and managing the Wagaku Kōdansho Institute. However, few people knew just how busy Hokiichi was as he worked hard to protect the dignity of blind people as members of society.

Under the Kansei Reforms instigated by Matsudaira Sadanobu, one of the shogunate's council of elders, the position of 'Zachū Torishimariyaku' ('Director of the Blind Guild') was established and, upon his appointment to this role, Hanawa Hokiichi proceeded with reforms to the disorganized blind society. Furthermore, he worked as 'Kanto Sōrokushoku', where he protected the interests of the blind in the Kantō region and also as a 'jūrō', one of the 10 top officials of the Tōdōza (the Blind Guild) that organized the blind community nationwide. The highest rank among these 10 was 'sōkengyō'*. In total, he served as sōkengyō for 29 years.

In particular, his role as 'Sōrokushoku' involved him moving his place of residence to the official Sōrokushoku mansion in Honjo Hitotsume and, in a time when transport was not well-developed, balancing his role there with his work at the Wagaku Kōdansho Institute, where he had been living, must have been very difficult.

Upon entering the Tōdōza, individuals started as 'shoshin' ('novice'). There were 73 ranks above that, the highest being 'kengyō'. Furthermore, the top 10 officials of 'kengyō' rank were known as 'jūrō' and the highest rank among them was 'sokengyō'.

Caption:
(P34)Lectures at the Wagaku Kōdansho Institute are open to all students, regardless of status, disabilities, age, wealth etc.

(P35)In February 1821 (Bunsei 4), Hokiichi is made 'sōkengyō' at the age of 75.

P36-37

No doubt he could have declined either of these roles as he was fully occupied with the editing and publication of the 'Gunsho Ruijū'. However, why did he take on the responsibilities of caring for the blind community, even though it took him away from his life's work of scholarship?

The background to this was the shogunate's policy of protecting the blind, particularly the system of high interest money lending (zatō-gane) exclusive to blind people.

Among the kengyō, some took advantage of this situation to conduct their business in a dishonest manner, leading to the whole blind community being viewed with contempt, as if they were all obsessed with money, like misers.

*

The following incident took place in Edo and became a topic of much discussion. A certain 'hatamoto' found himself in urgent need of funds and, despite being aware of the dangers involved, he had no choice but to borrow money through the 'zatō-gane' system. Unable to repay the loan on the due date and finding the severe collection methods unbearable, he fled in the night. As a result, his household was stripped of their status and they lost everything……. On the other hand, the 'kengyō' involved had their assets confiscated and were banished from Edo for charging excessively high interest rates and using aggressive collection methods.

The arrogant behaviour of these kengyō was criticized by public opinion, with it being said of them 'there are poor hatamoto who escape in the night and rich kengyō who indulge in luxurious lifestyles'. This led to an increase in discrimination against all blind people. Although his involvement with the Tōdōza placed heavy burdens on

Hokiichi, this relationship was of great importance to him until his dying days. In addition to upholding the tradition of the Tōdōza, whereby members offered each other mutual support, he also worked tirelessly to solve any issues that arose when any member might stray from that path, no matter how busy he was.

This was all done by Hokiichi because he recognized that, unless he held a high position within the Tōdōza, he couldn't carry out reforms to improve the social status of blind people. It was all in accordance with his motto, 'for the sake of all, for the sake of the future'*.

*'For the sake of all, for the sake of the future' was Hokiichi's catchphrase. Hokiichi, who was indifferent to career advancement and the accumulation of wealth, ultimately rose to the highest rank of 'sōkengyō' in a blind society where promotion up the ranks without financial resources was very difficult. Yet, the reason nobody ever spoke in envy of him lies in his sincere way of life, working hard 'for the sake of all, for the sake of the future'. People supported his activities, both spiritually and materially, upon witnessing this dedication, regardless of their status and position in society.

Caption:
    Hanawa Hokiichi, who passed on the ancient culture of Japan to later generations whilst blind, is a much admired figure for the blind and is also an ancestor who stands as a role model in life for all people. Young blind people look up to Hokiichi, who devoted his life for the sake of all, for the sake of the future.

P38-39

Conclusion (Connecting Hope To The Future)

Helen Keller, who said that Hanawa Hokiichi was her life's goal, reflected on her life and said the following, "Whenever I lost my way on my intended path in life, I would go out and walk in the woods. As I walk among the trees, the song of the roots, working hard in the dark depths of the soil, always comes to me. The roots of the trees cannot see the beautiful flowers they work so hard to produce, but they never complain." (Helen Keller, 'My Religion')

Helen played the role of the 'roots' supporting people's 'happiness' to the end of her days. Sometimes hailed as the 'saint of triple affliction' and at other times fiercely criticized as an 'unpatriotic citizen' for her opposition to war, her conviction of 'happiness for all' never wavered.

And so, what of Hanawa Hokiichi?

The four giants of Kokugaku (National Studies) would include Kada no Azumamaro, Kamo no Mabuchi, Motoori Norinaga and Hirata Atsutane, but there is no mention in that group of the Kokugaku scholar Hanawa Hokiichi. He chose a contrasting path to these four major scholars who were center stage in the field. He dedicated his entire life to providing accurate historical materials which would form a foundation to support the research of many other scholars. Hokiichi undertook this role because he believed someone had to shoulder it to advance the academic field as a whole.

Some 'Honorable Kengyō', said to be the equivalent in rank to a hatamoto, hoarded wealth, wore luxurious purple clothes and extravagant headgear to signify authority, held a kengyō staff as tall as themselves and paraded about the town accompanied by a retinue of attendants. On the contrary, people who were used to such displays must have felt a sense of familiarity and respect on seeing Hokiichi walking around the streets with the aid of his cane, always dressed in simple cotton clothes and carrying a stack of books wrapped in a cloth across his back.

Here, too, the similarities between these two great figures from Japan and America are evident at all time: 'Be without condescension or arrogance, live life authentically.'

The 21st century is said to be 'the century of coexistence' or 'the welfare century'. Maybe now is the time for us to take another look at the two great figures, Hanawa Hokiichi and Helen Keller, who always advocated for future generations with their philosophy of 'for the sake of all, for the sake of the future'.

People with disabilities have always been a minority in society. As members of the same society, it should be the desire and responsibility of each and every one of us living in the 21st century to realize a society where 'no one is left behind'. The aspirations of Hanawa Hokiichi and Helen Keller can be seen as a message to those of us living in the era of SDGs (Sustainable Development Goals)*.

*If things remain as they are, the Earth is in such a critical state that it won't be able to sustain itself. The Japanese government has stated, "The SDGs are international goals aimed at creating a sustainable and better world. Consisting of 17 goals and 169 targets, they pledge that no one on Earth will be left behind. SDGs are not only for developing countries but universal initiatives that advanced countries must also undertake, and Japan is actively committed to these goals."

Caption:
    Helen Keller and Hanawa Hokiichi face each other. Light is being shed on these two great figures.